Dear Parent:
Your child's love of reading st...

Every child learns to read in a different way and at his or her own speed. Some go back and forth between reading levels and read favorite books again and again. Others read through each level in order. You can help your young reader improve and become more confident by encouraging his or her own interests and abilities. From books your child reads with you to the first books he or she reads alone, there are I Can Read Books for every stage of reading:

SHARED READING
Basic language, word repetition, and whimsical illustrations, ideal for sharing with your emergent reader

BEGINNING READING
Short sentences, familiar words, and simple concepts for children eager to read on their own

READING WITH HELP
Engaging stories, longer sentences, and language play for developing readers

READING ALONE
Complex plots, challenging vocabulary, and high-interest topics for the independent reader

ADVANCED READING
Short paragraphs, chapters, and exciting themes for the perfect bridge to chapter books

I Can Read Books have introduced children to the joy of reading since 1957. Featuring award-winning authors and illustrators and a fabulous cast of beloved characters, I Can Read Books set the standard for beginning readers.

A lifetime of discovery begins with the magical words **"I Can Read!"**

Visit www.icanread.com for information
on enriching your child's reading experience.

I Can Read Book® is a trademark of HarperCollins Publishers.
Balzer + Bray is an imprint of HarperCollins Publishers.

Louise Loves Bake Sales
Text copyright © 2018 by Kelly Light
Illustrations copyright © 2018 by Kelly Light
All rights reserved. Manufactured in U.S.A.
No part of this book may be used or reproduced in any manner whatsoever without written permission except in the case of brief quotations embodied in critical articles and reviews. For information address HarperCollins Children's Books, a division of HarperCollins Publishers, 195 Broadway, New York, NY 10007.
www.icanread.com

ISBN 978-0-06-236365-7 (pbk.bdg.) — ISBN 978-0-06-236366-4 (trade bdg.)

The artist used many black Prismacolor pencils and Photoshop to create the illustrations for this book.

19 20 21   LSCC   10 9 8 7 6 5 4   ❖   First Edition

LOUISE
Loves
Bake Sales

Story by Laura Driscoll
Pictures by Kelly Light

BALZER & BRAY
An Imprint of HarperCollins*Publishers*

I love art!

I love this kind of art.

I love that kind of art.

I see art in everything!

Hmmm. . . .

Did you know food can be art?

We will make these cupcakes
into works of art.
We can make
a rainbow of cupcakes.

They look and smell so yummy.

But they need . . .

more COLOR!

We need red!

We need blue!

We need yellow!

We can mix colors to

make more colors.

Red and yellow

make orange!

Yellow and blue make green!

Blue and red

make purple!

Now we have all the colors—
ART!

What are you doing?

Oh no.

No more colors.

Just gray, gray, gray.

We cannot make a rainbow
with only gray!

Oh, well.

At least they taste good,

even if they don't look like art.

Wait. Look like Art . . . ?

That's it!

We can make them look like Art!

What do you think, Art?
I can't wait to show these
off at the bake sale!

All we need now is the perfect sign.

Aha!

I've got it!

You know what, Art?

Food is like art.

It does not always turn out

the way you planned.

Sometimes it turns out even better!